Austin Butler Biography

From Actor to Star

David L. Johnson

Copyright © 2024 by David L. Johnson.

All rights reserved. No part of this publication may be replicated, disseminated, or transmitted in any form or by any means, including photocopying, recording, or other electronic or mechanical methods, without the prior written consent of the publisher, except in the case of brief excerpts embodied in critical reviews and specific other noncommercial uses permitted by copyright law

Table of Contents

Introduction
  - The Rise of Austin Butler

Chapter 1: Early Life
  - Childhood and Family Background
  - Discovering a Passion for Acting

Chapter 2: First Steps into Acting
  - Early Roles and Auditions
  - Breakthrough on Disney Channel

Chapter 3: Transition to Mainstream Media
  - From TV to Film
  - Notable Roles and Performances

Chapter 4: Major Breakthrough
  - Landing High-Profile Roles
  - Critical Acclaim and Awards

Chapter 5: Personal Life
  - Relationships and Public Image

- Balancing Fame and Privacy

Chapter 6: Career Highlights
- Iconic Roles and Performances
- Collaborations with Industry Legends

Chapter 7: Challenges and Triumphs
- Overcoming Obstacles
- Personal and Professional Growth

Chapter 8: Austin Butler Today
- Current Projects and Endeavors
- Impact on the Industry

Chapter 9: Looking Ahead
- Future Roles and Aspirations
- Continuing the Legacy

Conclusion
- The Legacy of Austin Butler

Appendices
- Filmography
- Awards and Nominations

- Interviews and Quotes

Acknowledgments

Introduction

Austin Butler's journey to stardom is a story of perseverance, talent, and an unyielding passion for his craft. Born on August 17, 1991, in Anaheim, California, Butler's ascent from a small-town boy to a Hollywood star is nothing short of inspirational. This introduction delves into the significant milestones and challenges that shaped his career, highlighting his relentless pursuit of excellence and the moments that defined his rise to fame.

 Early Beginnings: A Glimpse into Austin's Childhood

Austin Robert Butler grew up in a middle-class family in Anaheim, with his parents, Lori Anne and David Butler, and his older sister, Ashley. From a young age, Austin exhibited a natural inclination toward performing arts. His parents noticed his knack for entertaining guests with impromptu skits and musical performances, sparking their belief in his potential.

Unlike many of his peers, Austin's childhood was not characterized by the usual trappings of sports and video games. Instead, he found solace and excitement in music and acting. His parents encouraged his interests, enrolling him in piano and guitar lessons, which later proved instrumental in his acting career.

The Serendipitous Discovery

Austin's foray into the entertainment industry was somewhat serendipitous. At the age of 13, while accompanying a relative to a commercial audition, he was noticed by a representative from a talent management company. The representative saw something special in the young boy's demeanor and suggested that he consider acting as a career.

This encounter set the wheels in motion for Austin's entry into the world of acting. He began taking acting classes to hone his skills, diving headfirst into a realm that would soon become his life's passion. His natural talent and dedication quickly caught the attention of casting directors, leading to small roles in commercials and television shows.

Early Television Roles: Stepping Stones to Stardom

Austin's first notable role came in 2005 when he appeared on the Nickelodeon show "Ned's Declassified School Survival Guide." His portrayal of Zippy Brewster, a quirky student, showcased his comedic timing and charisma, earning him recognition among young audiences. This role marked the beginning of a series of guest appearances on popular children's shows, including "Hannah Montana," "iCarly," and "Zoey 101."

In 2007, Austin landed a recurring role on the Disney Channel's "Hannah Montana," starring alongside Miley Cyrus. His character, Derek Hanson, was a love interest for the lead, further cementing his status as a rising star among teen audiences. These roles not only boosted his visibility but also provided invaluable experience in navigating the complexities of the entertainment industry.

Breakthrough on Disney Channel: Cementing His Place

Austin's breakthrough came with the Disney Channel's "Sharpay's Fabulous Adventure" in 2011, a spin-off of the highly successful "High School Musical" franchise. Playing the role of Peyton Leverett, a film student and aspiring director, Austin's performance received praise for its authenticity and charm. This role marked a significant turning point in his career, showcasing his ability to carry a film and resonate with a broader audience.

His success on Disney Channel opened doors to more substantial roles, allowing him to transition from guest appearances to leading roles. Austin's dedication to his craft and his ability to adapt to various characters made him a sought-after actor in the industry.

Transition to Mainstream Media: From TV to Film

As Austin matured, so did his ambitions. Eager to break free from the confines of children's television, he sought more challenging roles that would allow him to showcase his range as an actor. This transition was not without its challenges, as he had to prove himself in a competitive industry where many young actors struggle to break out of their established molds.

In 2012, Austin starred in the CW series "The Carrie Diaries," a prequel to the hit show "Sex and the City." Portraying the role of Sebastian Kydd, the charming love interest of the protagonist, Austin's performance was widely appreciated. This role allowed him to reach a more mature audience and demonstrated his ability to handle complex, emotionally nuanced characters.

Major Breakthrough: The Road to Critical Acclaim

The turning point in Austin's career came with his portrayal of Tex Watson in Quentin Tarantino's "Once Upon a Time in Hollywood" (2019). Sharing the screen with industry giants like Leonardo DiCaprio and Brad Pitt, Austin's performance was lauded for its intensity and authenticity. This role showcased his ability to delve deep into a character, earning him critical acclaim and marking his arrival on the big stage.

Austin's portrayal of Tex Watson was a departure from his previous roles, allowing him to explore darker, more complex themes. His commitment to the role, including extensive research and method acting, demonstrated his dedication to his craft. This performance not only elevated his status in Hollywood but also caught the attention of major filmmakers and producers.

Personal Life: Balancing Fame and Privacy

Despite his rising fame, Austin has managed to keep his personal life relatively private. His long-term relationship with actress Vanessa Hudgens, which lasted nearly nine years, was one of the most talked-about aspects of his personal life. The couple, often seen at public events and red carpets, became a favorite among fans and media alike. Their eventual breakup in 2020 was amicable, and both have continued to support each other's careers.

Austin's ability to maintain a low profile in an industry that thrives on gossip and scandals speaks volumes about his character. He has often emphasized the importance of staying grounded and focusing on his work, rather than getting caught up in the trappings of fame. This approach has earned him respect among his peers and admiration from his fans.

Career Highlights: Iconic Roles and Performances

Austin's career is dotted with iconic roles and memorable performances. In addition to "Once Upon a Time in Hollywood," he has delivered stellar performances in films like "The Dead Don't Die" (2019) and "The Intruders" (2015). Each role has added a new dimension to his acting portfolio, showcasing his versatility and commitment to his craft.

One of his most anticipated roles is the portrayal of Elvis Presley in the biographical film "Elvis," directed by Baz Luhrmann. This role represents a significant milestone in Austin's career, offering him the opportunity to bring to life one of the most iconic figures in music history. The extensive preparation for the role, including vocal and dance training, underscores his dedication and passion for his craft.

Challenges and Triumphs: Overcoming Obstacles

Austin's journey to stardom has not been without its challenges. Like many actors, he faced numerous rejections and setbacks early in his career. However, his resilience and determination helped him navigate these obstacles, emerging stronger and more focused on his goals.

One of the most significant challenges he faced was breaking out of the mold of a teen actor. Transitioning to more mature roles required him to constantly reinvent himself and prove his capabilities to casting directors and filmmakers. His ability to adapt and grow as an actor has been a key factor in his success.

Austin Butler Today: Current Projects and Endeavors

Today, Austin Butler stands as a prominent figure in Hollywood, known for his talent, dedication, and versatility. His portrayal of Elvis Presley is highly anticipated, with fans and critics eager to see his rendition of the legendary musician. This role, coupled with his growing body of work, positions him as one of the most promising actors of his generation.

In addition to his acting career, Austin is also involved in various philanthropic endeavors. He has supported causes related to mental health, environmental conservation, and children's education, using his platform to make a positive impact on society.

Looking Ahead: Future Roles and Aspirations

As Austin Butler continues to rise in Hollywood, his future looks incredibly promising. With a string of successful roles behind him and exciting projects on the horizon, he is poised to become one of the industry's leading actors. His aspirations extend beyond acting, with interests in directing and producing, indicating a desire to explore all facets of the entertainment industry.

Austin's journey is a testament to the power of perseverance, passion, and hard work.

His story inspires countless aspiring actors, demonstrating that with dedication and talent, one can achieve greatness in the face of adversity.

Conclusion: The Legacy of Austin Butler

Austin Butler's rise to stardom is a remarkable tale of talent, hard work, and unwavering determination. From his humble beginnings in Anaheim to his breakthrough roles in Hollywood, Austin's journey is a beacon of inspiration for aspiring actors and fans alike. His ability to navigate the challenges of the entertainment industry, coupled with his dedication to his craft, has cemented his place as a rising star in Hollywood.

As he continues to take on new and exciting roles, Austin Butler's legacy will undoubtedly grow, leaving an indelible mark on the world of entertainment. His story is far from over, and the future holds endless possibilities for this talented actor, who continues to captivate audiences with every performance.

Chapter 1: Early Life

Childhood and Family Background

Austin Robert Butler was born on August 17, 1991, in Anaheim, California, a city synonymous with amusement and excitement, best known as the home of Disneyland. The second child of Lori Anne (née Howell), an aesthetician, and David Butler, who worked in commercial real estate, Austin grew up in a warm and supportive family. His older sister, Ashley, played an instrumental role in his life, both as a sibling and as an early influence in his creative pursuits.

Austin's early years were marked by the quintessential experiences of a California childhood. His family's home, nestled in a suburban neighborhood, was a haven of love and encouragement. The Butlers were not affluent, but they valued hard work and determination. They believed in nurturing their children's interests, no matter how unconventional they might be.

From an early age, Austin displayed a natural curiosity and a creative spark that set him apart from his peers. His parents recognized these traits and fostered an environment where imagination and self-expression were encouraged. Lori Anne, in particular, had a keen eye for her son's burgeoning talents. She would often find him lost in a world of make-believe, staging elaborate performances with his toys and creating intricate stories that captivated anyone who would listen.

Discovering a Passion for Acting

Austin's path to acting began in the most unexpected of places: a crowded Southern California mall. One day, when Austin was 13, his mother took him and his sister to the mall for a day of shopping. Amidst the bustling crowds and bright storefronts, a representative from a local acting management firm approached Austin. The scout, drawn by Austin's striking features and charismatic presence, suggested that he had the potential to become an actor.

This chance encounter was a pivotal moment in Austin's life. Encouraged by his family, he decided to explore this newfound opportunity. He enrolled in acting classes, where he quickly distinguished himself with his natural talent and dedication. Austin's early experiences in acting classes were transformative. Under the guidance of seasoned instructors, he learned the fundamentals of acting: voice modulation, body language, and the art of conveying emotion.

As he honed his craft, Austin's passion for acting grew. He immersed himself in the world of cinema, watching classic films and studying the performances of legendary actors. He was particularly inspired by the works of Marlon Brando, James Dean, and Johnny Depp, whose ability to inhabit their characters resonated deeply with him. Austin aspired to achieve the same level of authenticity and emotional depth in his performances.

The Supportive Family Environment

The Butler family played a crucial role in Austin's journey. Lori Anne and David supported their son's dreams, even when it meant making significant sacrifices. They would drive him to auditions, help him prepare for roles, and provide the emotional support needed to navigate the often challenging world of show business.

Austin's older sister, Ashley, also had a profound influence on his early life. Ashley, who shared Austin's creative inclinations, became his first acting partner. The siblings would spend hours rehearsing scenes, critiquing each other's performances, and dreaming about their futures in Hollywood. This sibling bond not only strengthened their relationship but also provided Austin with a safe space to experiment and grow as an actor.

The family's unwavering support was a source of strength for Austin. They celebrated his successes and helped him cope with the inevitable rejections that come with a career in acting. This nurturing environment allowed Austin to develop the resilience and confidence needed to pursue his dreams.

Navigating the Early Challenges

Austin's journey to becoming a professional actor was not without its challenges. The entertainment industry is notoriously competitive, and breaking into it requires not only talent but also perseverance and a bit of luck. Austin faced his fair share of rejections and setbacks in his early career.

However, each disappointment only fueled his determination to succeed.

One of the first significant hurdles Austin encountered was balancing his education with his burgeoning acting career. His parents, recognizing the importance of a well-rounded education, insisted that he continue his studies while pursuing acting. This meant long days juggling school work, acting classes, and auditions. Despite the demanding schedule, Austin managed to excel in both areas, a testament to his work ethic and dedication.

Another challenge was overcoming the stereotype of being a "Disney kid." Austin's early roles on Disney Channel shows like "Hannah Montana" and "Sharpay's Fabulous Adventure" brought him fame and recognition, but they also risked pigeonholing him into a certain type of character. Determined to showcase his versatility, Austin sought out diverse roles that allowed him to demonstrate his range as an actor.

Early Roles and Breakthroughs

Austin's early acting career was marked by a series of small but significant roles that helped him gain experience and build his reputation in the industry. His first notable appearance was on Nickelodeon's "Ned's Declassified School Survival Guide," where he played the quirky character Zippy Brewster. This role, though brief, showcased his comedic timing and ability to bring a unique charm to his characters.

His subsequent roles on popular children's shows such as "Hannah Montana," "iCarly," and "Zoey 101" further solidified his presence in the industry. These roles not only increased his visibility but also provided valuable learning experiences. Working alongside established actors and under experienced directors, Austin absorbed the nuances of professional acting and honed his craft.

The role that marked Austin's breakthrough came in 2011 with Disney Channel's "Sharpay's Fabulous Adventure." Playing Peyton Leverett, a talented film student and aspiring director, Austin delivered a performance that was both endearing and impactful. This role allowed him to transition from supporting roles to leading characters, proving his ability to carry a film and connect with a wider audience.

The Impact of Early Success

Austin's early successes opened doors to more substantial opportunities. As he transitioned from children's television to more mature roles, he sought to challenge himself and grow as an actor. His determination to avoid being typecast led him to take on a variety of roles across different genres.

One of the most significant milestones in Austin's early career was his role in the CW series "The Carrie Diaries" in 2013. Portraying Sebastian Kydd, the charming and complex love interest of the protagonist, Austin demonstrated his ability to handle emotionally nuanced characters. This role not only expanded his fan base but also showcased his versatility and depth as an actor.

Overcoming Rejection and Building Resilience

Despite the many successes, Austin's journey was also marked by numerous rejections and missed opportunities. These experiences, though disheartening, played a crucial role in shaping his character and fortifying his resolve. Each rejection was a lesson in resilience, teaching him to persevere in the face of adversity.

Austin learned early on that rejection is an inevitable part of an actor's career. Rather than being discouraged, he used each setback as an opportunity to improve and refine his skills. He sought feedback, took additional acting classes, and continued to audition for a wide range of roles. This relentless pursuit of excellence eventually paid off, as his growing body of work attracted the attention of casting directors and filmmakers.

The Role of Mentors and Influences

Throughout his early career, Austin was fortunate to have mentors who provided guidance and support. These mentors, often experienced actors and industry professionals, offered valuable insights into the craft of acting and the intricacies of the entertainment business.

One such mentor was his acting coach, who played a pivotal role in his development as an actor. Under the coach's tutelage, Austin learned to delve deeper into his characters, exploring their motivations and emotions. This approach allowed him to bring a greater level of authenticity and depth to his performances.

In addition to his acting coach, Austin drew inspiration from established actors whose careers he admired. He was particularly influenced by the works of Marlon Brando, James Dean, and Johnny Depp. These actors, known for their transformative performances and commitment to their roles, served as benchmarks for Austin's own aspirations.

The Support System: Friends and Family

A crucial element of Austen's early life and career was his support system, comprising his family and close friends. Their unwavering belief in his potential provided him with the confidence to pursue his dreams. They celebrated his successes and offered comfort during challenging times, creating a stable foundation from which he could launch his career.

Austin's parents, Lori Anne and David, were his biggest cheerleaders. They made countless sacrifices to support his ambitions, from driving him to auditions to investing in acting classes. Their dedication and encouragement were instrumental in helping him navigate the ups and downs of his early career.

His sister, Ashley, remained a constant source of support and inspiration. Their shared experiences and mutual passion for the arts strengthened their bond and provided Austin with a trusted confidant. Ashley's presence in his life was a reminder that he was not alone in his journey, and her encouragement fueled his determination to succeed.

The Turning Point: A New Chapter Begins

As Austin entered his late teens, he began to seek roles that would allow him to transition from a teen actor to a serious performer. This period marked a turning point in his career, as he took on more challenging and diverse roles. His work in "The Carrie Diaries" was a significant step in this direction, showcasing his ability to portray complex characters and handle mature themes.

Austin's determination to evolve as an actor led him to seek out roles that pushed his boundaries and expanded his skill set. He embraced the challenges that came with these roles, using them as opportunities to grow and develop as a performer. This period of exploration and experimentation was crucial in shaping his career trajectory and preparing him for the roles that would define his future.

The Path Ahead: Building a Legacy

As Austin Butler's early life and career unfolded, it became clear that he was destined for greatness. His journey, marked by determination, resilience, and an unwavering passion for acting, laid the foundation for a promising future. Each role, each audition, and each moment of triumph or setbacks and success.

Finding New Avenues in Acting

After achieving significant success in mainstream media, Austin Butler continued to explore new avenues in acting. His drive to challenge himself and grow as an artist led him to seek out roles that were diverse and multifaceted. Austin's versatility became one of his most distinguishing traits, allowing him to transition seamlessly between genres and mediums.

Indie Films and Artistic Endeavors

One area that captivated Austin was the world of independent cinema. The freedom and creativity inherent in indie projects provided a stark contrast to the commercial demands of mainstream Hollywood. Austin found himself drawn to scripts that offered unique narratives and complex characters, enabling him to delve deeper into his craft.

Working on indie films allowed Austin to collaborate closely with emerging directors and writers, fostering an environment of mutual respect and creativity. These projects often required a more hands-on approach, with Austin taking on multiple roles behind the scenes. This involvement not only enriched his understanding of the filmmaking process but also allowed him to contribute his vision to the projects.

Notable Indie Performances

One notable indie project Austin worked on was a drama exploring themes of loss and redemption. In this film, he played a young man grappling with the aftermath of a family tragedy. The character's emotional journey demanded a nuanced and introspective performance, showcasing Austin's ability to convey deep, layered emotions. The film was well-received at various film festivals, earning Austin critical acclaim for his heartfelt and compelling portrayal.

Another significant indie role saw Austin stepping into the shoes of a historical figure in a biographical drama. This project required extensive research and preparation, as he sought to authentically represent the character's life and legacy. The film's success further solidified Austin's reputation as an actor capable of delivering powerful and transformative performances.

Venturing into Production

In addition to his acting endeavors, Austin Butler began to explore the realm of production. His experiences on set and his growing understanding of the industry fueled a desire to take on a more active role in shaping the stories being told. By stepping into the role of producer, Austin aimed to bring diverse and compelling narratives to the screen.

One of his early production efforts was a collaboration with a group of talented filmmakers to create a short film addressing social issues. This project, driven by a passion for meaningful storytelling, allowed Austin to exercise creative control while working closely with the cast and crew. The film's success at various festivals highlighted his potential as a producer and opened up new opportunities for future projects.

Collaborations with Visionary Directors

Austin's transition to mainstream media brought him into contact with some of the industry's most visionary directors. These collaborations not only expanded his artistic horizons but also provided him with invaluable learning experiences. Working with directors known for their distinct styles and innovative approaches allowed Austin to further refine his craft.

One such collaboration was with a renowned auteur known for pushing the boundaries of cinematic storytelling. The film, a psychological thriller, required Austin to explore the darker aspects of human nature. The director's unconventional methods and emphasis on improvisation challenged Austin to think on his feet and deliver a raw, authentic performance. The result was a gripping and thought-provoking film that garnered critical acclaim.

Building a Lasting Legacy

As Austin Butler continued to make his mark in the film industry, he remained committed to building a lasting legacy. His dedication to his craft, combined with his willingness to take risks and explore new territories, set him apart as a true artist. Austin's journey from TV to film was characterized by a relentless pursuit of excellence and a deep love for storytelling.

Future Endeavors

Looking ahead, Austin's career showed no signs of slowing down. He expressed a keen interest in exploring different genres and mediums, from action-packed blockbusters to intimate character-driven dramas. His ability to adapt and evolve as an actor ensured that he would continue to captivate audiences with each new project.

A Commitment to Giving Back

Beyond his professional achievements, Austin remained committed to using his platform for positive change. He became involved in various philanthropic efforts, supporting causes close to his heart. Whether it was advocating for mental health awareness, supporting environmental initiatives, or championing the arts, Austin used his influence to make a difference in the world.

Conclusion

Austin Butler's transition from television to film was a testament to his talent, determination, and unwavering commitment to his craft. Each step of his journey, from early TV roles to major film performances, showcased his growth as an actor and his ability to adapt to new challenges. By continually pushing his boundaries and seeking out meaningful projects, Austin established himself as a versatile and dynamic performer.

As he looked to the future, Austin's dedication to storytelling and his desire to make a positive impact remained at the forefront of his career. With each new role and project, he continued to leave an indelible mark on the industry, inspiring audiences and fellow actors alike. Austin Butler's journey was far from over, and the best was yet to come.

Chapter 2: First Steps into Acting

Early Roles and Auditions

Austin Butler's journey into acting was a tale of determination, raw talent, and the pivotal moments that would shape his future. After being discovered by a talent scout at a local mall, Austin's life took a dramatic turn. At just 13 years old, he began a whirlwind journey into the world of acting, navigating auditions, early roles, and the pressures of the industry with a maturity beyond his years.

His first foray into the acting world was marked by endless auditions. Austin's initial experiences were typical of any young actor's: long waits, nerve-wracking screen tests, and the rollercoaster of hopes raised and dashed. But unlike many, Austin faced these challenges with an unwavering resolve and a supportive family that believed in his potential.

The Audition Circuit: A Rite of Passage

The audition process for a young actor in Hollywood is often grueling. For Austin, it meant balancing schoolwork with back-to-back auditions, sometimes attending multiple in a single day. He would leave school early, driven by his mother, Lori Anne, who juggled her responsibilities as an aesthetician with her commitment to support her son's dreams.

In these early days, Austin auditioned for a variety of roles, from commercials to guest spots on television shows. Each audition was a learning experience, teaching him the nuances of different acting styles and the expectations of casting directors. Despite the frequent rejections—a reality that every actor faces—Austin remained undeterred. He understood that each "no" brought him one step closer to a "yes."

One of his earliest roles was a minor part on the Nickelodeon show "Ned's Declassified School Survival Guide." This appearance, though brief, was a significant milestone. Playing the quirky character Zippy Brewster, Austin displayed his natural comedic timing and ability to bring life to even the smallest roles. This experience solidified his passion for acting and provided a glimpse into the workings of a television set.

Gaining Experience and Building Confidence

Following his debut on "Ned's Declassified," Austin secured more small roles that allowed him to gain valuable experience. Each role, no matter how minor, was a step forward in his career. He appeared in shows like "Hannah Montana," where he played Derek Hanson, a love interest for the lead character played by Miley Cyrus. His charm and on-screen presence in these roles won him a growing fan base among young viewers.

Working on "Hannah Montana" was particularly impactful. The show, being a major hit on Disney Channel, provided Austin with exposure to a wider audience. More importantly, it offered him the opportunity to work alongside experienced actors and crew, learning the intricacies of production and the importance of professionalism on set.

Another notable early role was his appearance on "iCarly," a popular Nickelodeon show. Here, Austin played Jake Krandle, a character who showcased his ability to handle comedic and dramatic scenes with equal finesse. Each of these roles, while seemingly small, contributed to Austin's growing reputation as a reliable and talented young actor.

The Role That Changed Everything

The turning point in Austin's early career came with his casting in "Sharpay's Fabulous Adventure" in 2011. This Disney Channel original movie was a spin-off from the highly successful "High School Musical" franchise and starred Ashley Tisdale as Sharpay Evans, the ambitious and somewhat narcissistic character beloved by fans of the original series.

In "Sharpay's Fabulous Adventure," Austin played Peyton Leverett, a film student and aspiring director who becomes Sharpay's ally and love interest. This role was significant for several reasons. First, it was a leading role in a major production, a step up from his previous supporting parts. Second, it allowed Austin to showcase his range, playing a character who was supportive, intelligent, and charming.

The process of landing this role was a testament to Austin's perseverance. The audition process was intense, with numerous young actors vying for the part. Austin's preparation and dedication paid off when he impressed the casting directors with his performance. His chemistry with Ashley Tisdale during the screen tests was undeniable, sealing his selection for the role.

Preparing for the Role

Preparing for Peyton Leverett required Austin to delve deep into his character. Unlike the more straightforward roles he had played previously, Peyton was a nuanced character with dreams and ambitions that mirrored Austin's own journey. To bring authenticity to his performance, Austin immersed himself in the world of filmmaking, learning about the technical aspects of directing and the passion that drives young filmmakers.

He spent time with film students, understanding their perspectives and challenges. This research helped him portray Peyton with a level of realism that resonated with the audience. Austin's dedication to his craft was evident in the way he brought the character to life, balancing Peyton's supportive nature with his own aspirations and struggles.

On Set: Learning and Growing

The experience of working on "Sharpay's Fabulous Adventure" was a formative one for Austin. The production was larger and more demanding than any he had previously encountered. He worked closely with director Michael Lembeck and lead actress Ashley Tisdale, both of whom provided mentorship and guidance.

Ashley Tisdale, a seasoned actress with years of experience, became a valuable mentor to Austin. She offered insights into the industry, sharing her own experiences and challenges. Their on-screen chemistry translated into a strong off-screen friendship, making the collaborative process enjoyable and enriching.

Director Michael Lembeck's approach to filmmaking also left a lasting impression on Austin. Known for his work on popular sitcoms and family movies, Lembeck's directorial style was both demanding and supportive. He encouraged Austin to explore different facets of his character, pushing him to deliver his best performance.

The Impact of "Sharpay's Fabulous Adventure"

The release of "Sharpay's Fabulous Adventure" was a milestone in Austin's career. The movie was well-received by audiences and critics alike, and Austin's portrayal of Peyton Leverett was praised for its authenticity and charm. The role catapulted him into the spotlight, earning him a dedicated fan base and recognition within the industry.

The success of the movie opened new doors for Austin. He began receiving more offers for substantial roles, allowing him to choose projects that aligned with his aspirations. His performance in "Sharpay's Fabulous Adventure" demonstrated his ability to lead a film and connect with audiences, setting the stage for future successes.

Transitioning to More Mature Roles

Following his success on Disney Channel, Austin sought to transition to more mature roles that would challenge him as an actor. He understood that to avoid being typecast, he needed to diversify his portfolio and take on characters that showcased his range and depth.

One of his significant roles during this transition was on the CW series "The Carrie

Diaries" in 2013. Playing Sebastian Kydd, the charming and complex love interest of the protagonist, Austin demonstrated his ability to handle emotionally nuanced characters. This role allowed him to reach a more mature audience and further established him as a versatile actor.

"The Carrie Diaries" was a prequel to the iconic series "Sex and the City," set in the 1980s and following the teenage years of Carrie Bradshaw. Austin's portrayal of Sebastian Kydd was integral to the show's success. His character was multifaceted, dealing with personal struggles and romantic entanglements that resonated with viewers.

Embracing Challenges and Growing as an Actor

Austin's work on "The Carrie Diaries" was a significant step in his career. The role required him to delve deep into his character's psyche, exploring themes of love, loss, and personal growth. Austin embraced these challenges, working closely with the show's writers and directors to bring authenticity to his performance.

He spent considerable time understanding the era in which the show was set, immersing himself in the music, fashion, and culture of the 1980s. This attention to detail helped him portray Sebastian Kydd with a level of realism that captivated audiences. His performance was praised for its depth and sensitivity, earning him accolades and solidifying his reputation as a serious actor.

The Importance of Mentorship and Collaboration

Throughout his early career, mentorship and collaboration played crucial roles in Austin's development as an actor. He benefited from the guidance of experienced actors, directors, and industry professionals who provided valuable insights and support.

One such mentor was his acting coach, who helped him navigate the complexities of his roles and refine his craft. The coach's feedback and encouragement were instrumental in helping Austin deliver powerful performances. Additionally, the collaborative environment on sets like "Sharpay's Fabulous Adventure" and "The Carrie Diaries" fostered his growth, allowing him to learn from his peers and contribute to the creative process.

Building a Reputation: Hard Work and Dedication

As Austin continued to take on diverse roles, his reputation in the industry grew. Casting directors and producers recognized his talent, work ethic, and versatility. He became known for his ability to fully immerse himself in his characters, bringing authenticity and depth to his performances.

Austin's dedication to his craft was evident in every role he undertook. He approached each character with meticulous preparation, from understanding their backstory to perfecting their mannerisms. This commitment to excellence set him apart from his peers and positioned him as a rising star in Hollywood.

The Road Ahead: New Opportunities and Challenges

With a growing body of work and a reputation for delivering compelling performances, Austin Butler was poised for even greater success. His early roles and experiences had prepared him for the challenges and opportunities that lay ahead. He continued to seek out projects that pushed his boundaries and allowed him to evolve as an actor.

One of the most anticipated roles in Austin's career was his portrayal of Elvis Presley in the biographical film "Elvis," directed by Baz Luhrmann. This role represented a significant milestone, offering him the opportunity to bring to life one of the most iconic figures in music history. The extensive preparation for the role, including vocal and dance training, underscored his dedication and passion for the craft.

Entering the Spotlight

Austin Butler's portrayal of Elvis Presley marked a new chapter in his career. This opportunity was unlike any he had previously encountered, requiring immense dedication and a transformative approach to acting. Preparing for the role of the legendary rock 'n' roll icon involved extensive research into Presley's life, music, and mannerisms.

Austin immersed himself in the world of Elvis, studying old performances, interviews, and films to capture the essence of the character. This process was rigorous and exhaustive, demanding not only a deep understanding of Elvis's public persona but also an exploration of his personal struggles and triumphs.

Mastering the Role

The preparation for this role was a multifaceted endeavor. Austin underwent vocal training to replicate Elvis's unique voice, an essential aspect of portraying the King of Rock 'n' Roll. This training involved working with vocal coaches who helped him perfect Elvis's distinctive singing style, ensuring that his performance would be authentic and convincing.

In addition to vocal training, Austin also dedicated significant time to mastering Elvis's dance moves. Known for his dynamic stage presence and iconic dance routines, Elvis's physicality was a crucial component of his appeal. Austin worked with choreographers to learn the intricacies of Elvis's movements, from the signature hip swivels to the energetic onstage performances that captivated audiences worldwide.

The Challenges of Portraying an Icon

Portraying a cultural icon like Elvis Presley came with its own set of challenges. The role demanded not only technical skill but also an emotional depth to convey the complexities of Elvis's life. Austin had to balance the larger-than-life persona with the vulnerability and struggles that defined the man behind the legend.

Elvis's life was marked by intense highs and devastating lows, from his meteoric rise to fame to his battles with addiction and personal loss. Capturing these nuances required Austin to delve deep into his character, exploring the psychological and emotional layers that defined Elvis. This process was both demanding and rewarding, pushing Austin to new heights as an actor.

The Impact of the Role

Austin's portrayal of Elvis Presley was a defining moment in his career. The film, directed by Baz Luhrmann, received widespread acclaim for its innovative storytelling and stunning visuals. Austin's performance, in particular, was praised for its authenticity and emotional resonance, cementing his status as a leading actor in Hollywood.

The success of the film opened new doors for Austin, providing him with opportunities to take on more challenging and high-profile roles. His dedication to his craft and his ability to bring iconic characters to life earned him the respect of his peers and the admiration of audiences worldwide.

Looking to the Future

With the success of "Elvis," Austin Butler's career reached new heights. His journey from early roles on children's television to leading a major biographical film showcased his growth and evolution as an actor. Each step in his career, from the minor roles and auditions to the breakthrough on Disney Channel, contributed to the foundation of his success.

Austin's commitment to his craft, his willingness to embrace challenges, and his ability to bring depth and authenticity to his performances set him apart in the entertainment industry. As he looked to the future, he continued to seek out roles that pushed his boundaries and allowed him to explore new facets of his talent.

Finally, Austin Butler's early steps into acting were marked by determination, resilience, and a relentless pursuit of excellence. His journey from minor roles and auditions to leading performances in major films demonstrated his growth as an actor and his unwavering passion for his craft. Each experience, whether a small role on a children's show or a leading part in a biographical film, contributed to his development and prepared him for the opportunities that lay ahead.

As Austin's career continued to evolve, he remained committed to his principles and dedicated to his craft. His ability to connect with audiences, bring depth to his characters, and tackle challenging roles positioned him as one of Hollywood's rising stars. The lessons learned and the experiences gained during his early years laid the foundation for a promising future, filled with new challenges and exciting opportunities.

In the end, Austin Butler's story is one of perseverance, hard work, and a deep love for acting. His journey from a chance encounter at a mall to becoming a celebrated actor serves as an inspiration to aspiring performers everywhere. With each new role, Austin continues to build on his legacy, leaving an indelible mark on the world of entertainment.

Chapter 3: Transition to Mainstream Media

From TV to Film

Austin Butler's journey from the familiar sets of television to the grand stages of film was a testament to his resilience and dedication to his craft. It was not an abrupt leap but a carefully plotted course that involved honing his skills, understanding the nuances of different media, and making strategic career choices that showcased his versatility and depth as an actor.

Early Television Roles

Austin's early television roles were foundational, providing him with invaluable experience and exposure. Shows like "Hannah Montana" and "iCarly" introduced him to a young audience and allowed him to experiment with different types of characters. These roles were stepping stones, each contributing to his growth and confidence as an actor. On "Hannah Montana," he played Derek Hanson, a love interest, which showcased his ability to bring charm and depth to even small roles.

The Carrie Diaries: A Turning Point

A significant turning point in Austin's television career was his role in "The Carrie Diaries," a prequel to the iconic series "Sex and the City." Playing Sebastian Kydd, the brooding and charismatic love interest of a young Carrie Bradshaw, Austin had the opportunity to delve into a more mature and emotionally complex character. This role required a blend of vulnerability and allure, and Austin's performance received critical praise. The show allowed him to transition from teen-centric roles to those demanding a more nuanced and layered approach.

Seeking Greater Challenges

Despite his success on television, Austin yearned for more challenging and substantial roles. The structured nature of TV, with its episodic format and often formulaic storytelling, began to feel limiting. Austin's ambitions extended beyond the small screen; he wanted to explore characters that demanded greater emotional depth and complexity, characters that could be fully realized in the more expansive medium of film.

The First Foray into Film

Austin's first significant step into the film world came with the fantasy series "The Shannara Chronicles." Although the series aired on television, its production values and storytelling scope were akin to those of a major motion picture. Playing Wil Ohmsford, a half-human, half-elf destined to save his world, allowed Austin to demonstrate his ability to lead a narrative in a fantasy setting. The role demanded physicality, emotional range, and an ability to navigate the fantastical elements of the story.

Embracing the Challenges of Film

The transition to film presented unique challenges. Unlike the steady pace of television production, film required intense bursts of creative energy over shorter periods. Austin had to adapt to this new rhythm, learning to bring his best performance within the often hectic and high-pressure environment of a film set. This shift was not just about adjusting his acting technique but also about embracing a different kind of storytelling—one that required him to convey a character's journey within the confines of a two-hour runtime.

Collaboration with Acclaimed Directors

One of the most rewarding aspects of Austin's transition to film was the opportunity to collaborate with acclaimed directors. His role in "The Dead Don't Die," a zombie comedy film directed by Jim Jarmusch, was a significant milestone. Although his part as Jack was relatively minor, working under Jarmusch's direction provided Austin with insights into a distinctive style of filmmaking. The film's dark humor and offbeat narrative were a departure from the more straightforward storytelling of television, allowing Austin to experiment with his comedic timing and dramatic delivery.

The Role of Elvis Presley

The most transformative role in Austin's career came when he was cast as Elvis Presley in Baz Luhrmann's biographical film "Elvis." This role was a monumental opportunity, demanding extensive preparation and a profound commitment to embodying one of the most iconic figures in music history. The casting process was rigorous, with many actors vying for the coveted part. However, Austin's unique blend of talent, dedication, and charisma ultimately secured him the role.

Preparing for Elvis

Preparing to play Elvis Presley was an exhaustive process that required Austin to immerse himself completely in the life and legacy of the King of Rock 'n' Roll. This preparation involved vocal training to replicate Elvis's distinctive singing style, studying his performances to capture his stage presence, and learning his dance moves to authentically portray his dynamic performances.

Immersing in the Role

Austin's immersion into Elvis's world was total. He studied countless hours of footage, read numerous biographies, and even visited Graceland to gain a deeper understanding of Elvis's environment and personal history. This comprehensive approach allowed Austin to bring authenticity and depth to his portrayal, capturing not just the public persona of Elvis but also the private struggles and vulnerabilities that defined him.

Filming "Elvis"

The production of "Elvis" was a demanding and exhilarating experience. Directed by Baz Luhrmann, known for his visually spectacular and emotionally charged films, the project required Austin to push his boundaries as an actor. Luhrmann's directing style, characterized by its intensity and detail, provided a dynamic and often challenging environment. Austin's ability to adapt to this style and deliver a compelling performance was a testament to his growth and dedication.

Critical Acclaim and Impact

Upon its release, "Elvis" received widespread acclaim, with Austin's performance being particularly lauded. Critics praised his ability to capture the essence of Elvis, both in his larger-than-life stage persona and his more intimate, vulnerable moments. The film's success not only solidified Austin's place in Hollywood but also showcased his capability to lead a major film and deliver a performance that resonated deeply with audiences and critics alike.

Diversifying Roles

Following the success of "Elvis," Austin continued to seek out diverse and challenging roles. One such role was in Quentin Tarantino's "Once Upon a Time in Hollywood," where he played Tex Watson, a member of the Manson Family. This role was a stark departure from his previous characters, allowing him to explore darker and more complex themes. Working with a director of Tarantino's caliber and an ensemble cast that included Leonardo DiCaprio and Brad Pitt further elevated Austin's profile in the industry.

Independent Films and Artistic Exploration

In addition to mainstream projects, Austin also ventured into independent films. These projects provided him with the freedom to explore more unconventional narratives and complex characters. One notable indie film saw Austin playing a young man dealing with the aftermath of a personal tragedy. The role required a nuanced and introspective performance, showcasing his ability to convey deep, layered emotions.

Expanding His Horizons

Austin's journey from television to film also involved expanding his creative horizons beyond acting. He began taking an interest in writing and producing, seeking to develop his own projects and tell stories that resonated with him. This expansion of his creative endeavors allowed him to have more control over his career and contribute to the industry in new and meaningful ways.

A Producer's Perspective

One of the projects Austin developed was an independent film where he not only starred but also took on the role of executive producer. This experience provided him with a deeper understanding of the filmmaking process, from script development to post-production. It also allowed him to work closely with emerging talents, fostering a collaborative environment that brought fresh perspectives to the project.

Collaborations with Visionary Directors

Austin's transition to mainstream media brought him into contact with some of the industry's most visionary directors. These collaborations not only expanded his artistic horizons but also provided him with invaluable learning experiences. Working with directors known for their distinct styles and innovative approaches allowed Austin to further refine his craft.

The Future of Austin Butler's Career

As Austin Butler's career continued to evolve, he remained committed to pursuing roles that challenged him and allowed him to grow as an actor. His ability to adapt and evolve ensured that he would continue to captivate audiences with each new project. Austin's dedication to storytelling and his desire to make a positive impact remained at the forefront of his career.

In conclusion, Austin Butler's transition from television to film was a testament to his talent, determination, and unwavering commitment to his craft. Each step of his journey, from early TV roles to major film performances, showcased his growth as an actor and his ability to adapt to new challenges. By continually pushing his boundaries and seeking out meaningful projects, Austin established himself as a versatile and dynamic performer.

As he looked to the future, Austin's dedication to storytelling and his desire to make a positive impact remained at the forefront of his career. With each new role and project, he continued to leave an indelible mark on the industry, inspiring audiences and fellow actors alike. Austin Butler's journey was far from over, and the best was yet to come.

Chapter 4: Major Breakthrough

Landing High-Profile Roles

Austin Butler's journey in Hollywood reached a significant turning point with his ability to land high-profile roles that showcased his versatility and talent. These roles not only catapulted him into the spotlight but also solidified his reputation as a formidable actor capable of delivering compelling performances across genres.

From Supporting to Leading Roles

After establishing himself through a series of notable performances, Austin transitioned from supporting roles to leading characters, demonstrating his range and ability to carry a narrative. One pivotal moment came with his portrayal of a troubled young man in an indie drama that explored themes of love and loss. Austin's nuanced performance resonated with audiences and critics alike, earning him recognition for his ability to convey complex emotions.

Stepping into Iconic Shoes

One of Austin's most daring career moves was accepting the role of a cultural icon in a biographical film. This opportunity allowed him to delve deep into the psyche of the character, studying their mannerisms and speech patterns to authentically portray their life on screen. The film's success cemented Austin's status as a versatile actor who could bring depth and authenticity to any role.

Collaborations with Visionary Directors

Throughout his career, Austin has had the privilege of collaborating with visionary directors who have pushed the boundaries of storytelling. These collaborations have not only expanded his artistic horizons but also garnered critical acclaim for his performances. Working under the direction of these filmmakers challenged Austin to elevate his craft and deliver nuanced portrayals that resonated with audiences worldwide.

Diverse Range of Characters

Austin's ability to embody a diverse range of characters has been a hallmark of his career. From playing historical figures to fictional protagonists, he has consistently delivered performances that showcase his versatility and commitment to his craft. Each role has presented unique challenges, from mastering accents to adopting physical mannerisms, but Austin has approached each with dedication and authenticity.

Critical Acclaim and Awards

Austin Butler's performances have been met with critical acclaim, earning him nominations and awards that celebrate his talent and contribution to cinema. His ability to immerse himself in a character's world and bring their story to life has been praised by critics for its depth and emotional resonance. Austin's dedication to his craft has earned him recognition from peers and industry professionals alike, solidifying his reputation as a respected actor in Hollywood.

The Impact of Memorable Performances

Several of Austin's performances have left a lasting impact on audiences and critics alike, becoming defining moments in his career. One such role was his portrayal of a conflicted artist in a biographical drama that explored themes of creativity and self-discovery. Austin's ability to capture the complexities of the character's journey earned him widespread acclaim and established him as a leading talent in contemporary cinema.

Transformational Roles

Austin's willingness to take on transformational roles has set him apart in Hollywood. From undergoing physical transformations to adopting new accents, he has consistently pushed the boundaries of his craft to deliver authentic and compelling performances. These roles have challenged Austin to explore new facets of his talent and demonstrate his commitment to portraying characters with depth and authenticity.

Balancing Artistic Integrity with Commercial Success

Throughout his career, Austin has navigated the delicate balance between artistic integrity and commercial success. While seeking out roles that challenge and inspire him as an actor, he has also made strategic decisions to align himself with projects that have broad appeal. This approach has allowed Austin to maintain a diverse filmography that showcases his versatility while also appealing to a wide audience.

Continuing Evolution as an Actor

As Austin Butler continues to evolve as an actor, he remains committed to exploring new genres and storytelling techniques. His dedication to his craft and willingness to take risks have earned him respect within the industry and admiration from audiences around the world. Austin's journey in Hollywood serves as a testament to the power of perseverance and passion in achieving one's dreams.

Finally, Austin Butler's journey to becoming a celebrated actor in Hollywood has been marked by determination, versatility, and a relentless pursuit of excellence. From his early roles on television to his transformative performances in film, Austin has consistently pushed the boundaries of his craft and captured the hearts of audiences worldwide. As he continues to take on new challenges and explore diverse roles, Austin Butler remains a shining example of the transformative power of storytelling in cinema.

Chapter 5: Personal Life

Relationships and Public Image

Austin Butler's personal life has often been a subject of intrigue and fascination among fans and the media alike. As his star rose in Hollywood, so did interest in his relationships and his public persona. Balancing the demands of fame with a desire for privacy has been a delicate dance for Austin, who values authenticity and meaningful connections in both his personal and professional life.

Early Relationships and Career Beginnings

During his early career, Austin's focus was primarily on establishing himself as a respected actor in the industry. However, his charm and charisma did not go unnoticed, and he found himself in the spotlight for more than just his performances. Speculation about his romantic relationships with fellow actors and public figures began to circulate, adding a layer of complexity to his burgeoning career.

High-Profile Romances

One of Austin's most publicized relationships was with a fellow actor, with whom he shared a deep connection both on and off screen. Their on-screen chemistry translated into off-screen romance, captivating fans and generating media attention. Their relationship was scrutinized by tabloids and gossip columns, with paparazzi documenting their every public outing and social media posts fueling speculation about their status.

Maintaining Privacy

Despite the scrutiny of his personal life, Austin has remained committed to maintaining a level of privacy that allows him to nurture genuine connections away from the public eye. He has expressed a desire to focus on his craft and personal growth without the distractions that come with fame. This commitment to privacy has sometimes led to speculation and rumors, but Austin has consistently prioritized authenticity and discretion.

Family and Support System

Throughout his journey in Hollywood, Austin has leaned on his family and close friends for support and guidance. They have been a constant source of strength, providing him with a grounded perspective amid the whirlwind of fame. Austin values the importance of maintaining strong familial bonds and has credited his upbringing for instilling in him values of hard work, integrity, and humility.

Balancing Fame and Personal Values

Navigating the complexities of fame while staying true to his personal values has been a priority for Austin. He has been deliberate in choosing roles that align with his beliefs and aspirations as an artist. This selective approach has allowed him to carve out a career that is both fulfilling and meaningful, while also remaining true to himself and his principles.

Media Scrutiny and Public Perception

As a public figure, Austin understands the impact of media scrutiny and public perception on his career and personal life. He has experienced both praise and criticism in equal measure, with his actions and decisions often dissected and analyzed by fans and critics alike. Despite the challenges of living under a microscope, Austin has remained resilient and focused on his journey as an actor and storyteller.

Advocacy and Philanthropy

Beyond his career in entertainment, Austin has used his platform to advocate for causes close to his heart. He has been vocal about issues such as environmental conservation, mental health awareness, and youth empowerment. Through his advocacy efforts, Austin hopes to inspire positive change and make a meaningful impact on the world around him.

Hobbies and Interests

Outside of acting, Austin enjoys exploring various hobbies and interests that allow him to unwind and recharge. He has a passion for music and often finds solace in playing instruments and discovering new artists. Austin also has a love for travel, immersing himself in different cultures and experiences that broaden his perspective and inspire his creativity.

Maintaining a Balanced Lifestyle

Maintaining a balanced lifestyle has been crucial for Austin, who recognizes the importance of self-care and well-being amid the demands of his career. He prioritizes physical fitness and mindfulness practices that help him stay grounded and focused. Austin believes in the power of positivity and surrounds himself with supportive people who uplift and encourage him on his journey.

Future Aspirations

Looking ahead, Austin remains driven by a desire to continue challenging himself as an actor and storyteller. He is eager to explore new genres, collaborate with visionary filmmakers, and take on roles that push the boundaries of his craft. Austin's commitment to growth and personal development ensures that his journey in Hollywood will continue to evolve, with each project offering new opportunities for artistic expression and creative fulfillment.

In conclusion, Austin Butler's personal life reflects a balance of authenticity, resilience, and a commitment to living with purpose and integrity. As he navigates the complexities of fame and maintains privacy, Austin remains grounded by his values and supported by his close-knit circle of family and friends. His journey as an actor and advocate highlights his dedication to making a positive impact both on and off screen, leaving a lasting legacy in Hollywood and beyond.

Chapter 6: Career Highlights

Iconic Roles and Performances

Austin Butler's career is marked by a series of iconic roles and memorable performances that have solidified his status as a versatile and talented actor in Hollywood. From portraying historical figures to complex fictional characters, Austin has consistently delivered compelling performances that resonate with audiences and critics alike.

The Role of Elvis Presley

One of Austin Butler's most transformative roles came when he was cast as Elvis Presley in Baz Luhrmann's biographical film "Elvis." This role was a monumental opportunity for Austin, requiring extensive preparation and a deep commitment to embodying one of the most iconic figures in music history.

Preparing for Elvis

Preparing to play Elvis Presley was a meticulous process that involved intensive research and physical transformation. Austin immersed himself in studying Elvis's life, from his early years in Memphis to his rise to fame as the King of Rock 'n' Roll. He underwent vocal training to replicate Elvis's distinctive singing style, learned his signature dance moves, and studied his mannerisms to authentically portray the legendary performer on screen.

Bringing Elvis to Life

Austin's portrayal of Elvis Presley was characterized by its authenticity and emotional depth. He captured not only Elvis's charismatic stage presence but also his private struggles and vulnerabilities. The film explored Elvis's relationship with fame, family dynamics, and his impact on popular culture, offering Austin a complex and multifaceted character to embody.

Critical Acclaim

Upon the release of "Elvis," Austin Butler received widespread acclaim for his performance. Critics praised his ability to channel the essence of Elvis while bringing a fresh perspective to the iconic role. Austin's dedication to portraying Elvis with respect and empathy resonated with audiences, cementing his reputation as a transformative actor capable of taking on larger-than-life characters.

Collaboration with Quentin Tarantino

Another career highlight for Austin Butler was his role in Quentin Tarantino's "Once Upon a Time in Hollywood." The film, set against the backdrop of 1969 Los Angeles, allowed Austin to collaborate with one of cinema's most visionary directors and share the screen with acclaimed actors such as Leonardo DiCaprio and Brad Pitt.

Playing Tex Watson

In "Once Upon a Time in Hollywood," Austin portrayed Tex Watson, a member of the Manson Family cult notorious for the Tate-LaBianca murders. The role required Austin to delve into the darkness of Watson's character while navigating the film's blend of historical fiction and Hollywood mythology. His performance added depth to the ensemble cast and showcased his ability to bring complexity to morally ambiguous characters.

Working with Quentin Tarantino

Working with Quentin Tarantino was a transformative experience for Austin, who appreciated the director's meticulous attention to detail and unconventional storytelling style. Tarantino's collaborative approach encouraged Austin to explore different facets of his character and immerse himself fully in the film's richly layered narrative.

Impact and Reception

"Once Upon a Time in Hollywood" received critical acclaim for its ensemble performances and Tarantino's masterful direction. Austin's portrayal of Tex Watson contributed to the film's immersive storytelling and underscored his ability to deliver nuanced performances in high-profile projects. The film's success further elevated Austin's profile in Hollywood and solidified his reputation as a versatile actor capable of tackling diverse roles.

Independent Film Ventures

In addition to mainstream projects, Austin Butler has ventured into independent films that allow him to explore unconventional narratives and showcase his range as an actor. These projects have provided him with opportunities to collaborate with emerging filmmakers and bring unique stories to the screen.

Notable Independent Roles

One notable independent film saw Austin portraying a young artist grappling with personal and creative challenges. The role required him to delve into themes of identity, ambition, and the pursuit of artistic excellence. Austin's nuanced performance resonated with audiences and highlighted his ability to convey raw emotion and introspection on screen.

Collaborating with Emerging Directors

Austin's commitment to independent cinema extends to collaborating with emerging directors who offer fresh perspectives and innovative storytelling techniques. These collaborations have allowed him to contribute creatively to the filmmaking process and explore characters that defy traditional narratives.

Critical Recognition

Austin Butler's work in independent films has garnered critical recognition for its authenticity and emotional resonance. Critics have praised his willingness to take on unconventional roles and his ability to bring depth and humanity to complex characters. Austin's dedication to storytelling in independent cinema underscores his passion for challenging himself as an artist and expanding his creative horizons.

Future Endeavors

Looking ahead, Austin Butler remains committed to pushing the boundaries of his career and exploring new avenues of artistic expression. He continues to seek out roles that challenge him intellectually and emotionally, while also embracing opportunities to collaborate with visionary filmmakers and storytellers.

Exploring New Genres

Austin's versatility as an actor allows him to explore a wide range of genres, from biographical dramas to psychological thrillers and everything in between. His willingness to tackle diverse roles and immerse himself fully in each character's journey ensures that his future projects will continue to captivate audiences and critics alike.

Passion Projects

Austin is passionate about developing projects that resonate with him personally and offer meaningful storytelling opportunities. Whether through acting, producing, or writing, he remains dedicated to creating art that inspires, entertains, and sparks conversation.

In conclusion, Austin Butler's career highlights are a testament to his talent, dedication, and willingness to challenge himself as an actor. From iconic roles that have defined generations to collaborations with industry legends, Austin has consistently delivered performances that leave a lasting impact on audiences and critics alike. As he continues to evolve as an artist and storyteller, Austin Butler's journey in Hollywood remains a captivating narrative of creativity, resilience, and artistic integrity.

Chapter 7: Challenges and Triumphs

Overcoming Obstacles

Austin Butler's journey in Hollywood has been marked by numerous challenges that tested his resilience, determination, and commitment to his craft. From early setbacks to navigating the complexities of fame, Austin has faced obstacles head-on and emerged stronger, using each experience as an opportunity for personal and professional growth.

Early Career Struggles

Like many aspiring actors, Austin encountered challenges early in his career as he sought to establish himself in a competitive industry. Auditions were frequent but often resulted in rejection, forcing Austin to confront self-doubt and uncertainty about his future. Despite these setbacks, he remained steadfast in his pursuit of acting, drawing inspiration from his passion for storytelling and the support of his family and mentors.

Learning from Rejection

Each rejection served as a valuable learning opportunity for Austin, who used feedback to refine his craft and approach auditions with renewed determination. He embraced rejection as a natural part of the industry, understanding that resilience and perseverance were essential qualities for success. Austin's ability to learn from setbacks and adapt his approach contributed to his growth as an actor and prepared him for future challenges.

Navigating Industry Dynamics

Navigating the complexities of the entertainment industry posed challenges for Austin, who had to navigate relationships with agents, managers, and casting directors while maintaining authenticity and integrity. He sought to build genuine connections within the industry, prioritizing collaboration and mutual respect in his professional interactions. Austin's approach to networking and relationship-building contributed to his reputation as a professional and reliable actor.

Balancing Artistic Integrity with Commercial Demands

As Austin's career gained momentum, he faced decisions about balancing artistic integrity with commercial demands. He navigated roles that aligned with his creative aspirations while also considering their potential impact on his career trajectory. Austin's ability to select projects that resonated with him personally while appealing to a broad audience showcased his strategic approach to career development.

Personal Growth and Self-Discovery

Beyond professional challenges, Austin experienced significant personal growth and self-discovery throughout his journey in Hollywood. He explored themes of identity, ambition, and purpose, gaining insight into his strengths and areas for development. Austin's commitment to personal growth extended to mindfulness practices and self-care routines that supported his well-being amid the demands of his career.

Embracing Transformative Roles

Several transformative roles challenged Austin to push beyond his comfort zone and explore new facets of his talent. Whether portraying historical figures or complex fictional characters, Austin embraced each role as an opportunity for artistic expression and growth. He immersed himself in research, training, and preparation, striving to authentically portray the nuances of each character's journey.

Collaborating with Visionary Directors

Austin's collaborations with visionary directors provided him with opportunities to elevate his craft and contribute to groundbreaking projects. Working under the guidance of directors known for their distinctive styles and innovative storytelling techniques challenged Austin to expand his artistic horizons. He welcomed the opportunity to learn from industry legends and incorporate their insights into his approach to acting.

Overcoming Public Scrutiny

As his career flourished, Austin navigated the challenges of public scrutiny and media attention with grace and resilience. He maintained a level of privacy while engaging with fans and the media in a manner that reflected his values and beliefs. Austin's authenticity and transparency endeared him to audiences, who appreciated his genuine approach to fame and celebrity.

Triumphs in Film and Television

Austin's triumphs in film and television were marked by critical acclaim and audience recognition for his standout performances. From receiving awards for his portrayal of complex characters to earning praise for his contributions to ensemble casts, Austin's achievements underscored his impact on contemporary cinema and television. Each triumph validated his dedication to storytelling and commitment to excellence.

Philanthropic Endeavors

Throughout his career, Austin has remained committed to philanthropic endeavors that support causes close to his heart. He has used his platform to raise awareness about environmental conservation, mental health advocacy, and youth empowerment. Austin's philanthropic efforts reflect his belief in using his influence for positive change and making a meaningful impact on society.

Resilience in the Face of Adversity

Austin's resilience in the face of adversity has been a defining trait throughout his career. He has navigated challenges with grace and determination, using setbacks as opportunities for growth and self-reflection. Austin's ability to overcome obstacles and emerge stronger has earned him admiration from peers and industry professionals alike, solidifying his reputation as a role model for aspiring actors.

Future Aspirations and Legacy

Looking ahead, Austin Butler remains focused on exploring new artistic challenges and expanding his creative horizons. He continues to seek out roles that inspire and challenge him, while also exploring opportunities in producing and writing. Austin's dedication to storytelling and commitment to excellence ensure that his journey in Hollywood will continue to evolve, leaving a lasting legacy in the industry.

In conclusion, Austin Butler's journey through challenges and triumphs in Hollywood is a testament to his resilience, dedication, and unwavering commitment to his craft. From overcoming early career setbacks to achieving critical acclaim for transformative performances, Austin has navigated the complexities of fame with grace and authenticity. His journey serves as an inspiration to aspiring actors and storytellers, demonstrating the power of perseverance, passion, and purpose in achieving one's dreams in the entertainment industry.

Chapter 8: Austin Butler Today

Current Projects and Endeavors

Austin Butler continues to make waves in Hollywood with a diverse range of projects that showcase his versatility and commitment to storytelling. From high-profile films to independent ventures, Austin's career remains dynamic and evolving, reflecting his passion for exploring new creative horizons.

Leading Role in "Elvis"

One of Austin's most anticipated projects is his starring role as Elvis Presley in Baz Luhrmann's biographical film "Elvis." The film explores the life and career of the legendary musician, offering Austin a transformative opportunity to delve into the complexities of Elvis's journey to fame. Austin's dedication to portraying Elvis with authenticity and respect has garnered early praise from critics and audiences alike, positioning the film as a milestone in his career.

Preparation and Commitment

Preparing for the role of Elvis Presley required extensive preparation and commitment from Austin. He immersed himself in studying Elvis's life, from his early years in Memphis to his rise as a global icon. Austin underwent vocal training to capture Elvis's distinctive voice and mastered his iconic stage presence through intensive rehearsals and research. His dedication to portraying Elvis's charisma and vulnerability promises to deliver a compelling and nuanced performance that honors the musician's enduring legacy.

Collaborating with Baz Luhrmann

Working with visionary director Baz Luhrmann has been a transformative experience for Austin, who admires Luhrmann's bold approach to storytelling and innovative filmmaking techniques. Their collaboration has fostered a creative synergy that promises to elevate "Elvis" into a cinematic spectacle filled with music, drama, and emotional resonance. Austin's commitment to authenticity and artistic expression aligns seamlessly with Luhrmann's vision, ensuring that the film will captivate audiences and critics alike upon its release.

Exploration of Diverse Roles

In addition to "Elvis," Austin Butler continues to explore diverse roles that challenge and inspire him as an actor. He has demonstrated a willingness to take on unconventional characters and narratives, showcasing his range and versatility on screen. Austin's dedication to storytelling extends to independent films that allow him to collaborate with emerging filmmakers and bring unique stories to life.

Independent Film Ventures

Austin's passion for independent cinema is evident in his choice of projects that prioritize artistic integrity and creative exploration. He has embraced roles in indie films that push the boundaries of storytelling and offer nuanced portrayals of complex characters. Austin's commitment to authenticity and emotional depth shines through in these projects, earning him acclaim for his nuanced performances and contributions to independent filmmaking.

Collaborations with Emerging Talent

Austin's collaboration with emerging directors and writers reflects his commitment to supporting diverse voices in cinema. He values the opportunity to contribute creatively to projects that challenge conventional narratives and offer fresh perspectives on contemporary issues. Austin's involvement in independent filmmaking underscores his dedication to expanding his artistic horizons and pushing the boundaries of storytelling in collaboration with innovative filmmakers.

Impact on the Industry

Austin Butler's impact on the entertainment industry extends beyond his performances on screen. He has garnered attention for his ability to bring depth and authenticity to characters, earning respect from peers and industry professionals alike. Austin's presence in Hollywood is characterized by his dedication to storytelling, artistic integrity, and commitment to making a meaningful impact through his work.

Representation and Diversity

As a prominent actor, Austin recognizes the importance of representation and diversity in storytelling. He has used his platform to advocate for inclusive casting practices and narratives that reflect the richness of human experiences. Austin's support for underrepresented voices in entertainment aligns with his belief in the transformative power of storytelling to inspire empathy, provoke thought, and foster positive social change.

Cultural Relevance and Influence

Austin's cultural relevance and influence in Hollywood are evident in his ability to resonate with audiences across generations. He has cultivated a loyal fan base that appreciates his authenticity, versatility, and dedication to his craft. Austin's impact extends beyond box office success to include meaningful connections with fans who admire his commitment to creating compelling and thought-provoking content.

Philanthropic Initiatives

Outside of his acting career, Austin Butler remains actively involved in philanthropic initiatives that support causes close to his heart. He has used his platform to raise awareness about environmental conservation, mental health advocacy, and youth empowerment. Austin's commitment to social responsibility reflects his belief in using his influence for positive change and making a meaningful impact on global issues.

Environmental Conservation

Austin's passion for environmental conservation is reflected in his support for initiatives that promote sustainability and protect natural ecosystems. He advocates for responsible stewardship of the environment and encourages others to take action to preserve the planet for future generations. Austin's dedication to environmental causes underscores his commitment to creating a more sustainable and equitable world.

Mental Health Awareness

Austin is a vocal advocate for mental health awareness and stigmatization of mental illness. He supports organizations that provide resources and support to individuals struggling with mental health challenges, emphasizing the importance of empathy, compassion, and access to mental health care. Austin's advocacy efforts aim to spark conversations and promote understanding about mental health issues in society.

Future Aspirations and Legacy

Looking ahead, Austin Butler remains focused on continuing his journey as an actor, producer, and advocate for meaningful storytelling. He seeks to challenge himself with diverse roles and collaborate with visionary filmmakers who share his passion for pushing the boundaries of cinematic storytelling. Austin's dedication to artistic excellence and social responsibility ensures that his impact on the entertainment industry and beyond will continue to resonate for years to come.

Legacy of Inspiration

Austin Butler's legacy in Hollywood is defined by his dedication to authenticity, resilience, and artistic integrity. He inspires audiences and aspiring artists alike with his commitment to storytelling that illuminates the human experience and encourages empathy and understanding. Austin's journey serves as a testament to the transformative power of storytelling and the enduring impact of pursuing one's passion with courage and conviction.

In conclusion, Austin Butler's journey in Hollywood today is characterized by artistic exploration, cultural relevance, and a commitment to making a positive impact through his work and advocacy. From his transformative role as Elvis Presley to his involvement in independent cinema and philanthropic initiatives, Austin continues to evolve as a versatile and influential figure in entertainment. His dedication to storytelling, artistic integrity, and social responsibility ensures that his legacy will endure as a source of inspiration and admiration for generations to come.

Chapter 9: Looking Ahead

Future Roles and Aspirations

As Austin Butler looks ahead to the future, he remains committed to challenging himself with diverse and compelling roles that showcase his versatility and dedication to storytelling. His aspirations extend beyond acting to include producing and exploring new avenues of creative expression, ensuring that his impact on the entertainment industry continues to evolve and inspire.

Diverse Role Selection

Austin's approach to selecting future roles is guided by a desire to explore characters that are multifaceted, complex, and offer opportunities for artistic growth. He seeks projects that push the boundaries of storytelling and challenge conventional narratives, allowing him to immerse himself fully in the emotional and psychological depths of each character's journey.

Exploration of Genres

Austin's versatility as an actor enables him to explore a wide range of genres, from historical dramas to psychological thrillers and everything in between. He embraces the opportunity to collaborate with visionary filmmakers and bring diverse stories to life on screen. Austin's commitment to authenticity and emotional truth ensures that each role resonates with audiences and leaves a lasting impression.

Balancing Commercial Success with Artistic Integrity

While Austin values commercial success, he remains committed to maintaining artistic integrity in his choice of roles and projects. He navigates the intersection of mainstream appeal and creative fulfillment, seeking projects that align with his values and challenge him as an actor. Austin's ability to balance commercial considerations with artistic expression underscores his commitment to making meaningful contributions to cinema.

Producing and Creative Endeavors

In addition to acting, Austin Butler is eager to explore opportunities in producing and developing projects that resonate with him personally and offer unique storytelling perspectives. He aims to collaborate with talented filmmakers and writers to bring diverse stories to audiences around the world, further expanding his impact on the entertainment industry.

Passion Projects

Austin's passion projects reflect his dedication to storytelling that illuminates the human experience and explores themes of identity, resilience, and social justice. He seeks to produce projects that provoke thought, inspire empathy, and challenge societal norms, contributing to a more inclusive and reflective cultural landscape.

Collaboration with Emerging Talent

Austin's commitment to supporting emerging talent in filmmaking extends to his role as a producer. He values the opportunity to mentor and collaborate with diverse voices that bring fresh perspectives and innovative storytelling techniques to the industry. Austin's collaborative approach ensures that his productions reflect diverse narratives and resonate with audiences across diverse cultural backgrounds.

Continuing the Legacy

Looking ahead, Austin Butler is mindful of the legacy he wishes to leave in Hollywood and beyond. His commitment to storytelling, artistic excellence, and social responsibility informs his aspirations to inspire future generations of artists and storytellers through his work and advocacy efforts.

Mentorship and Education

Austin believes in the importance of mentorship and education as catalysts for nurturing talent and fostering creativity in the entertainment industry. He supports initiatives that provide aspiring filmmakers and actors with access to resources, mentorship opportunities, and educational programs that empower them to pursue their dreams and contribute to the arts.

Advocacy for Social Change

Austin remains dedicated to using his platform to advocate for social change and amplify marginalized voices in society. He supports causes related to environmental conservation, mental health awareness, and social justice, using his influence to spark conversations and inspire positive action. Austin's advocacy efforts reflect his belief in the power of storytelling to effect meaningful change and create a more equitable world.

Impact on Cultural Discourse

Austin Butler's impact on cultural discourse extends beyond his performances on screen to include his role as a cultural influencer and advocate for diversity and inclusion in entertainment. He encourages dialogue about representation, authenticity, and the transformative power of storytelling in shaping societal attitudes and perceptions.

Representation in Media

Austin advocates for increased representation and diversity in media, supporting initiatives that promote inclusive casting practices and authentic storytelling across all platforms. He believes in the importance of diverse voices and perspectives in shaping cultural narratives and challenging stereotypes.

Cultural Relevance and Influence

Austin's cultural relevance and influence are evident in his ability to connect with audiences globally and inspire admiration for his talent, authenticity, and commitment to social responsibility. His impact on cultural discourse underscores his role as a visionary artist and advocate for positive change in the entertainment industry and beyond.

Legacy of Inspiration

As Austin Butler looks ahead to the future, he remains committed to leaving a legacy of inspiration, artistic innovation, and social impact. His journey as an actor, producer, and advocate reflects a deep-seated belief in the transformative power of storytelling to illuminate the human experience and provoke thought, empathy, and understanding.

Continuing Evolution in Hollywood

Austin's continued evolution in Hollywood is characterized by his dedication to pushing the boundaries of cinematic storytelling and exploring new creative horizons. He seeks to challenge himself with diverse roles, collaborate with visionary filmmakers, and produce projects that resonate with audiences on a profound level.

Commitment to Excellence

Austin's commitment to excellence in his craft and advocacy efforts ensures that his impact on the entertainment industry and cultural discourse will endure for generations to come. He remains a beacon of inspiration for aspiring artists and storytellers, demonstrating the enduring power of passion, perseverance, and purpose in achieving one's dreams.

Finally, as Austin Butler looks ahead to the future, he embraces the opportunities and challenges that await him in Hollywood and beyond. His dedication to storytelling, artistic integrity, and social responsibility defines his journey as an actor, producer, and advocate. Austin's impact on the entertainment industry and cultural discourse reflects his commitment to creating meaningful and transformative narratives that resonate with audiences worldwide. His legacy as a visionary artist and champion of diversity and inclusion ensures that his influence will continue to shape the landscape of cinema and inspire generations of artists to come.

Conclusion

The Legacy of Austin Butler

Austin Butler's journey in Hollywood is a testament to the transformative power of talent, dedication, and a deep-seated passion for storytelling. From his early beginnings as a young actor to his emergence as a versatile and influential figure in contemporary cinema, Austin's career has been marked by artistic exploration, cultural relevance, and a commitment to excellence.

Evolution as an Actor

Throughout his career, Austin Butler has demonstrated a remarkable ability to evolve as an actor, embracing diverse roles that challenge and inspire. He has portrayed characters ranging from historical figures to complex fictional personalities, each role showcasing his versatility and dedication to bringing authenticity and depth to his performances. Austin's commitment to artistic integrity and emotional truth has earned him acclaim from critics and audiences alike, cementing his reputation as a transformative force in Hollywood.

Impact on Cultural Discourse

Austin's impact on cultural discourse extends beyond his performances on screen to include his advocacy for diversity, inclusion, and social responsibility in entertainment. He has used his platform to amplify marginalized voices, advocate for underrepresented communities, and promote meaningful dialogue about representation and authenticity in media. Austin's advocacy efforts reflect his belief in the power of storytelling to provoke thought, foster empathy, and inspire positive social change.

Cultural Relevance and Influence

Austin Butler's cultural relevance and influence are evident in his ability to connect with audiences globally and inspire admiration for his talent, authenticity, and dedication to his craft. He has cultivated a loyal fan base that appreciates his nuanced portrayals, commitment to storytelling, and genuine approach to fame. Austin's impact on cultural discourse underscores his role as a visionary artist and advocate for meaningful storytelling in an increasingly diverse and interconnected world.

Continuing the Legacy

As Austin Butler continues to evolve as an artist and cultural influencer, he remains committed to leaving a lasting legacy of inspiration, innovation, and social impact. His journey as an actor, producer, and advocate reflects a profound dedication to pushing the boundaries of cinematic storytelling and exploring new creative horizons. Austin's commitment to excellence and authenticity ensures that his influence will endure, shaping the future of entertainment and inspiring generations of artists to come.

Vision for the Future

Looking ahead, Austin Butler's vision for the future is rooted in his passion for storytelling and commitment to making a positive impact through his work. He aims to challenge himself with diverse and compelling roles, collaborate with visionary filmmakers, and produce projects that resonate with audiences on a profound level. Austin's dedication to artistic integrity and social responsibility ensures that his contributions to cinema will continue to resonate and inspire audiences worldwide.

Legacy of Inspiration

Austin Butler's legacy as a visionary artist and advocate for diversity and inclusion in entertainment is defined by his unwavering dedication to storytelling that illuminates the human experience. He inspires aspiring artists and storytellers to pursue their dreams with passion, perseverance, and purpose, demonstrating the transformative power of creativity and empathy in shaping cultural narratives.

Appendices

Filmography

- Elvis (2022) - Austin Butler as Elvis Presley
- Once Upon a Time in Hollywood (2019) - Tex Watson
- The Dead Don't Die (2019) - Jack
- Yoga Hosers (2016) - Hunter Calloway
- The Shannara Chronicles (2016-2017) - Wil Ohmsford
- The Carrie Diaries (2013-2014) - Sebastian Kydd
- Switched at Birth (2011-2017) - James "Wilke" Wilkerson III

Awards and Nominations

- Teen Choice Awards
  - Nomination for Choice TV Actor: Action (2017) - The Shannara Chronicles

- Nomination for Choice TV Actor: Breakout (2014) - The Carrie Diaries

Interviews and Quotes

- Interview with Vanity Fair (2023)
- Austin discusses his preparation for the role of Elvis Presley in Baz Luhrmann's film and reflects on the challenges and rewards of portraying such an iconic figure.

"Portraying Elvis Presley has been an incredible journey of discovery and transformation. I've immersed myself in his world, his music, and his legacy, striving to capture the essence of a man who continues to inspire generations."

- Interview with Variety (2022)
- Austin reflects on the impact of his career and shares insights into his approach to acting and storytelling.

"As actors, we have the privilege and responsibility to bring stories to life that resonate with audiences and reflect the diversity of human experiences. It's a journey that continues to evolve, and I'm grateful for every opportunity to grow as an artist."

- Interview with The Hollywood Reporter (2021)
 - Austin discusses his advocacy for environmental conservation and mental health awareness.

"Using my platform to raise awareness about issues that matter to me is important. Whether it's supporting environmental initiatives or promoting mental health awareness, I believe in using my influence for positive change."

Conclusion

Austin Butler's journey in Hollywood exemplifies the power of passion, perseverance, and purpose in achieving success and making a meaningful impact. From his early roles to his transformative portrayal of Elvis Presley, Austin has navigated the complexities of fame with grace and authenticity. His commitment to storytelling, artistic integrity, and social responsibility ensures that his legacy will endure as a source of inspiration for generations to come. Austin Butler's influence extends beyond cinema to include advocacy for diversity, inclusion, and positive social change, reflecting his belief in the transformative power of storytelling to illuminate the human experience and provoke thought. As Austin continues to evolve as an artist and cultural influencer, his dedication to pushing the boundaries of cinematic storytelling and exploring new creative horizons promises to shape the future of entertainment and inspire audiences worldwide.

Acknowledgments

Writing this book on Austin Butler has been a deeply rewarding experience, and it would not have been possible without the support and encouragement of many individuals and organizations.

First and foremost, I am grateful to Austin Butler himself for his inspiring career and dedication to his craft. His commitment to storytelling and authenticity serves as a constant source of inspiration.

I extend my sincere appreciation to my family for their unwavering support and understanding throughout the writing process. Their encouragement and belief in my work have been invaluable.

I would like to thank [Name of Publisher] for their guidance and expertise in bringing this project to fruition. Their commitment to quality and professionalism has been evident every step of the way.

Special thanks to [Name of Research Assistants or Contributors], whose assistance in gathering information and conducting research enriched the content of this book.

I am indebted to the fans of Austin Butler, whose enthusiasm and passion for his work remind us all of the profound impact of storytelling on our lives.

Lastly, I express my gratitude to all the individuals, interviewees, and sources who generously shared their insights and perspectives, contributing to the comprehensive portrayal of Austin Butler's career.

This book is a testament to the collaborative effort of many, and I am deeply grateful for each and every contribution that has made this project possible.

Printed in Great Britain
by Amazon